How to Sell For Beginners

The First Guide You Need To Make Your First Sale

TABLE OF CONTENTS

Introduction

Chapter One: Why You Need To Research Your Market Before Creating Your Product

Chapter Two: What To Do After Your First Sale

Chapter Three: Why Making Your First Sale Online Is So Important To Your Success

Chapter Four: The Ultimate Guide On How To Start Your Own Online Business

Chapter Five: Enjoying Your First Sale

Chapter Six: 4 Crucial Things You Need When Building Your List

Conclusion

Introduction

I want to thank you and congratulate you for downloading the book, *"How to Sell For Beginners: The First Guide You Need To Make Your First Sale"*.

This book contains proven steps and strategies on how to How to Make Your First Sale as a Beginner - The Best Way Possible.

Internet marketing is not an easy thing to do. Many tried and failed. Even their very first try on how to make your first sale online is a forgettable experience. But then there are also those whose experiences are worth bragging about. They were able to con□uer the challenges that come their way. They are the one that other people should emulate. What could be their secrets of success?

Internet business is an equal opportunity for everyone. Knowledge is vast in this world. You don't even have to pay a penny for information if you want to. But if you want to become really successful in internet marketing business, you need to learn how to invest. There free things in the internet but the best knowledge are offered for a certain cost. People who have learn the system the best way did it with a high price to pay. This includes not only monetary value but also their effort and emotional strength.

If you want to make your first money online, you have to be ready to face the challenge. Readiness alone is not enough. You have to learn through every experiences, most of them painful and frustrating. But knowing what's ahead together with the knowledge of every actions involved is a good way of ensuring success.

To make your very first sale you need to learn the best knowledge available.

Thanks again for downloading this book, I hope you enjoy it!

CHAPTER ONE

WHY YOU NEED TO RESEARCH YOUR MARKET BEFORE CREATING YOUR PRODUCT

Market research is a key element to product creation. After all, if there is no market for the product, you will have no buyers, and no buyers means no sales and no sales means no money on your pocket. Too many people create a product first and then look for the market, the issue with this is that there may not be a market, or you may create your entire campaign directed at a sub-niche or part of the niche that doesn't buy, or worse yet gets offended by what you created.

Instead of wasting your valuable time and money, the best method to create a product is to do your research beforehand. Once you know there is a market and what the market wants you can customize and create a product to solve their urgent issue and create for yourself a product perfect for those hungry buyers.

Another thing to look at with your chosen niche is how the products are typically delivered. Is everything in PDF format? Is there any reason you can see for only those certain formats being used. For example, creating PDF's to help blind adults get the help they need, isn't going to work too well, but creating an audio product or a physical product written in braille will. You need to step inside the mind of the potential buyer and see what mediums that they would use and why.

You'll also want to look at the competition and see how they are marketing the finished product. Are they using article marketing, video, PPC or another means. If you find all competition is using PPC you should take it that perhaps other methods don't work, and if you don't have the budget or ability to market the way the niche buys, then again, it is better to find out before you make the product then after you have completed it and are wondering why no one is buying.

Once you've completed your market research and fully understand the targeted buyer, then and only then should you begin your product creation. Doing it the other way around is almost a sure way to fail. Sure you may have one of those one-hit wonders that fit outside the realm of normal results, but it is not exactly what you want to be banking on.

Starting a New Business? Here are the Accounting Decisions You Need to Make

Starting a new business is exciting, but in that excitement are a lot of decisions to be made. Out of all them all, the financial backbone of your business needs to be seriously taken into consideration. A large part of that are the accounting decisions you will need to make. When starting a new business, you will want to spend some time on the following areas:

The type of organization your business is. Are you a sole proprietor or are you in business with someone else? Will you organize as a partnership or as a corporation? Limited liability companies are the newest form of entity - is this form right for your business? Choosing an organizational type will determine what federal and state income forms to file. For example, a corporation may need to file annual reports in the state of the incorporation.

The fiscal year of your business. Most businesses use the calendar year, but that may not be the proper choice for your business. For tax purposes, many businesses choose a different beginning and ending date than the January through December calendar year.

The accounting method for your business. Are you going to use a cash or accrual method of accounting? The cash method is easier for startup companies, however, if you have inventory - the IRS may force you to use accrual.

You will have to decide if your business will follow GAAP (generally accepted accounting principles) or Tax Basis for financial statement disclosures. Your banker may prefer one over the other.

The method of valuing inventory for your business. Accounting principles allow many methods, like LIFO (last in first out), FIFO (first in first out), and Lower of Cost or Market. You will need to choose the right method for your business.

Financial records for your business. You have a lot of choices here! Are you going to use paper ledger sheets to record sales and purchases? Are you going to keep track of income and expense using a computer program? Some bookkeeping software has the ability to integrate your data with an accounting professional, thus saving you money. You will need to decide the best method for your business.

Feeling a little overwhelmed? All of the above can be much easier if you have an accounting professional to guide you. This is another decision you will need to make. Will you hire an in-house accounting clerk or will you outsource your accounting needs?

Unfortunately, too many new businesses skimp on setting their accounting backbone up correctly at the start of their business. The financial backbone needs to be strong, as it is the support of your entire venture. You can get expert help in these initial stages, and decisions, in setting up a new business, so that your business starts off right.

Starting a new business is exciting! If you take the time to talk with your accounting professional about the above decisions, you will help ascertain the best possible beginnings for your business.

<u>When starting a new business, you will want to spend some time on the following areas:</u>

- ❖ *The type of organization your business is.*
- ❖ *The fiscal year of your business.*
- ❖ *The accounting method for your business.*
- ❖ *The method of valuing inventory for your business.*
- ❖ *Financial records for your business.*

CHAPTER TWO

WHAT TO DO AFTER YOUR FIRST SALE

For far too many marketers, the ultimate objective of their business is to generate a product sale. Of course, generating a sale is terrific as it puts money into your bank or PayPal account but the critical thing to understand is that the first sale should be nothing more than that, a first.

It is a sale that indicates that your prospect is willing to spend money on a product or service that is suitably well matched to their re□uirements but as far as putting money into your bank account is concerned, you must view this initial sale as nothing more than the very first step.

By making this purchase, your new customer has made a commitment to your business, and as this commitment can be measured in monetary terms, it is one of significant value. Nevertheless, if you stop at this point, you are leaving a huge amount of money on the table because there is so much more that you can and should do at this point.

The key thing to understand as you read this chapter is that many marketers focus on the idea of bringing more targeted traffic to their site as their primary way of increasing their business income by selling more online.

However, if you follow what you're going to read over the next few pages, you can generate significantly increased levels of income without ever seeing one additional visitor arrival on your site.

Of course, if you can increase visitor numbers at the same time as putting the strategy into place, you will make money from both actions, but the crucial fact is, in order to make more money by selling more online, you just need to have a system that minimizes the amount of 'leakage' that so many online businesses suffer.

To get an idea of where there is extra money to be made, think about the last time you went into McDonald's.

After you ordered your Big Mac, what was the first thing they did? Did they just leave it at that, or did they ask you whether you want fries with that? Of course, they asked you whether you wanted fries and the chances are that you said 'yes'.

Did they stop there? No, of course they didn't, they asked you whether you wanted to supersize your meal and whether you wanted a Coke with it. When you confirmed that you did, the next question was whether you wanted a regular or a large Coke, right?

All down the line, they are offering additional choices and options with which you can optimize your experience and customize your order to match your own exact re uirements. They are therefore offering you a service of value and uality whilst of course generating additional income for their employers at exactly the same time.

This simple practice of offering the option to customize or optimize your order is worth millions of dollars to McDonald's every day, and (crucially) in order to generate these additional millions of dollars, they do not need one additional customer to walk through the door of any of their outlets! In marketing terms, this process of introducing additional products or services into the sales process is often known as upselling but this is a phrase that sometimes has negative connotations. Consequently, in order to appreciate the true significance of this practice for your business, I would suggest that you change your own perception of what this process really represents.

Whilst some people see upselling as being evil in some way, this is simply not the case at all. After all, you wouldn't accuse the assistant who asked you whether you wanted fries with your big Mac of doing anything wrong other than offering you an additional service or experience.

You should view your own business in exactly the same way. Once you have completed the initial sale to your new customer, you should then offer additional products or services that will enhance the experience attached to buying your initial product.

This is in fact a great example of giving your customers exactly what they want. It is after all reasonable to assume that having spent money on the initial product, they want to be able to use that product in the most effective and efficient way possible, so why not do whatever you can to help them achieve what they want?

If therefore you are in a position to provide additional resources or products that will help them to get the most out of what they have just spent their money on, you are offering them the ability to optimize their experience in exactly the same way that the assistant was doing in the fast-food scenario highlighted earlier.

For example, say that you have just sold a $47 e-book to your new customer that teaches them what the best natural treatments for their acne problem are. Of course, the reason that they have bought this particular e-book is because they have an acne problem and they want to treat it naturally without resorting to chemical-based pharmaceutical drugs.

Now imagine that many of the natural remedies that you suggest in your guide are based on home recipes that you create using herbs and other natural household substances like yogurt.

How useful would it be to your new customer if you created a series of videos that demonstrated exactly how you make these natural homemade treatments? Although by following the instructions in your manual, they may be working to some kind of recipe in the same way that you would if you were attempting to create a gourmet meal, you probably know from your own experience that following a written recipe is never the easiest way of learning how to make a gourmet meal properly.

However, if you were able to offer them a series of video demonstrations that show exactly how to make your natural acne treatment 'potions' rather than offering only your e-book, these videos would clearly make it easier for that customer to use the product that they just bought from you.

What To Do After Your First Sale

- ❖ *Provide additional resources or products that will help them to get the most out of what they have just spent their money on.*
- ❖ *Have a system that minimizes the amount of 'leakage' that so many online businesses suffer.*

CHAPTER THREE

WHY MAKING YOUR FIRST SALE ONLINE IS SO IMPORTANT TO YOUR SUCCESS

Making your first sale on the internet is a pretty amazing feeling. When you make that first sale you finally know for a fact that making money online is possible.

Until you have made that first sale you may even have a little bit of doubt in your head because you have never actually made any money online.

Making your first sale online will help you to get rid of that doubt and it will help you move ahead in your business much ⬜uicker. When you make that sale it will not only prove that online marketing works, but it will also give you an idea of what it takes to actually make sales.

Don't Give Up

I remember when I was just starting to learn about online marketing. I tried probably 10 different marketing strategies before I found 1 that worked for me. After I finally found a strategy that worked for me, it still took months for me to get my first lead!

There was a time in the beginning that I felt so overwhelmed with information that I didn't know what to do or who to listen to. I was trying to learn 10 different strategies at once, and none of them were working for me.

The Turning Point

Everything changed for me when I began to focus on just 1 marketing strategy. I ignored all the other strategies and advice from others and just focused on this one strategy until I started to see results.

After I decided to focus on this one strategy I finally got my first lead...and then my first sale.

"It is better to be exceptional at 1 thing than to be mediocre at 10"

Make It A Goal To Get That First Sale

If you haven't made money online, then you should make it your goal to make that first sale as soon as possible. Making your first sale will reveal so much to you that you don't know now.

When you make that sale it will also encourage you to make more sales and it will boost your confidence as well. In the world of online marketing there are relatively few people who actually make money.

Plus-You will get an idea of what it takes to make sales online. Before you make a sale you may not know how many leads it takes to get a sale. Once you know this information it will make it far easier for you to plan your business out.

For some reason it makes things a lot easier when you have an idea of what to expect. Before you get that sale you don't really know how many leads will have to get.

The sad part about this is that some people might quit before making that first sale. They may have 15 or 20 leads and decide to ☐uit because they haven't seen a sale yet.

It Is A Numbers Game

When you make a sale it gives you priceless insight into the online marketing game. You will now know how many leads you need for a sale and you can make a gameplan for your business.

For example if you know it takes 30 leads to make a sale, then you can plan your business and marketing strategy to fit those numbers.

Then you can hit those numbers and even exceed your expectations if you continue to follow up with your prospects. The simple fact is that the more leads you get in your business the more sales you will make over time.

You may get a lead that is interested in what you have to offer, but it might just be a bad time for that person to buy. If you keep following up with your leads, then you will catch that person at a better point in their life and they will buy from you.

Having an online business is hard in the beginning stages, but once you get going it becomes easier and more profitable. The quickest way to get to the next stage in your business is to get that first sale... even if you have to do some paid advertising to make it happen.

SureFire Sales Tips for Making Your First Sale

I ask you, who does not want to make money? If you're one of those considering the possibility of selling online, do not worry it's not that complicated. So where does your first Internet sale come from? First of all you are going to need a decent reliable computer and importantly a reliable Internet connection, this is important and of course you need something to sell.

If you already have a reliable computer and a good connection, then the next ☐uestion is: "Where should I sell?" There are a number of online sales sites where you can list your item for sale. Some charge a fee for registration, while some charge only if you sell your item. Ensure you carry out thorough research on the site you decide to list with. You need to know their policy on charging and also their terms and conditions also check the site security to ensure that you are protected against fraud.

So you have chosen your selling site and set up your account so what's next? You need to write a description of your item. Photograph it so the add looks professional. The description of the item and quality of your photo's is very important, you will sell if the listing is of good quality and won't sell if it is not. You are new to this and need to start off with a good add and a positive feedback. Your add description should read if your item is new or used, and what are its uses or purposes. You need a detailed product description. You need to decide what price you are going to sell the item for, as a guide it might be good to use 50% of retail cost and see how the sale goes. Keep checking the status of your add to see if there are any ☐uestions about the item.

It is always a good idea to check how much the item is selling for on the site, Do a bit of research on the website you have chosen and see how much other sellers are asking for it. Buyers want items in new or good condition at a good price. Be honest about the condition of the item, this will ensure that you do receive good feedback.

I hope these tips prove to be useful, your first sale should come soon.

Sales Tips for Making Your First Sale

- ❖ *You need to write a description of your item.*
- ❖ *Photograph it so the add looks professional.*

- ❖ *The description of the item and quality of your photo's is very important, you will sell if the listing is of good quality and won't sell if it is not.*
- ❖ *You are new to this and need to start off with a good add and a positive feedback.*
- ❖ *Your add description should read if your item is new or used, and what are its uses or purposes.*
- ❖ *You need a detailed product description.*
- ❖ *You need to decide what price you are going to sell the item for, as a guide it might be good to use 50% of retail cost and see how the sale goes.*
- ❖ *Keep checking the status of your add to see if there are any ☐uestions about the item.*

CHAPTER FOUR

THE ULTIMATE GUIDE ON HOW TO START YOUR OWN ONLINE BUSINESS

If you're looking for information on how to start your own online business, there are a number of ways that you can easily do so. Whether you're thinking of selling a product or offering a service, the Internet can provide you with a wide market that you can cater to. Starting an online may seem easy enough, but becoming really successful in it is a completely different matter. So if you want to gain an advantage over all the other online businesses out there, then here are a few things that you might want to keep in mind.

Treat it as your full-time job

In order to achieve success you have to always put your maximum effort into your endeavor. Sure, having an online business can be a very enticing idea since it allows you to work from home, but this means that you need to work doubly hard since you'll basically be responsible for paying a salary to yourself. Many people who have their own businesses at home find it difficult at first to set business time apart from family time. So it's important that you keep focused by recognizing that there are boundaries between the two.

Stick to a niche

Another factor that can increase your chances of becoming successful is your capacity to plan just what type of product or services you'll be offering and if there a specific target market that you're after. By setting out plans this early in the game, you'll be able to research on different marketing techni ues that will enable you to reach your target audience much more effectively. You need to study the profile of your regular customer to know what type of message, should you communicate to him or her so that you'll be able to get more sales. Most experts believe that sticking to a niche is a great way that you'll be able to earn profits on a regular basis.

Types of online businesses you can get into

But first, before getting into the technical details on how to start your own online business, you should first decide on which type of online venture you want to get into. As mentioned earlier, there are a lot of options that you can choose from so make sure that you select a business opportunity that has the potential to become profitable, and at the same time, enjoyable for you as well. Here are the top 5 ideas:

- Affiliate marketing
- Online store (eBay)
- Article marketing
- Blogging + ad sense program
- Freelancing

Don't forget to choose an online venture that will be able to match your own set of skills so that you can run the business much smoothly.

So there you have it; the ultimate guide on how to start your own online business. Always remember that it's best to be prepared before jumping into tasks at hand to make sure that you do your research first before diving into any business decisions. Though it may seem a bit confusing at first, don't get easily intimidated, as there are always experts that you can turn to for advice.

How to Make Your First Product Launch a Success - A Step-by-Step Guide

Launching a product successfully on the internet can be difficult. Depending on the niche that you're targeting for your product, competition can be fierce. Regardless, there are certain steps that you should take to ensure that your product launch is a successful one.

The first step in the process is market research. It's important to know what your market needs and is looking for. Usually there is some sort of need or problem that people have in a niche market. A successful product is one that helps alleviate that problem and makes their lives easier.

Once you've done the market research, you need to put a plan of action into place. Plan every single step of your launch from beginning to end. You want to be prepared as much as possible to ensure a smooth and successful launch.

A pre-launch would be a good idea at this point. You want to get as much feedback from others as possible to know what they like and don't like about the product. Gathering testimonies is a good idea. You can use these testimonies on your website when it's time for the actual launch to take place and your product is available to everyone.

Now that you have feedback on your product and have maybe tweaked it a bit, you want to find partners to help promote your product. The best way to get a lot of exposure for your product is to contact the big names in your niche that will help spread the word about your launch. At this point you'll have a launch date set and have marketing materials handy for your partners to help promote the launch and your product.

The only thing left to do is wait for the official launch of your product. Once your product is launched, you'll want to track sales and see where your customer's are coming from to help better your marketing efforts. Keep promoting your product, and with the help of your partners, you should have a □uite successful product launch.

Motivations to Keep in Mind to Know How to Make Your First Sale on the Internet

No matter what role you play or what kind of product you sell online, making that first sale is both challenging and wonderful. Everything else that you know about business and the strategies you have saved up for this moment remain a theory until you have sealed that first deal. You can memorize all the theories in the book, recite all the mantras, discuss business strategies, and ace any cross-examination but these cannot be proven until you actually see a sale coming in the cash register.

Questions like, will anyone like what I'm selling? Will anyone ever notice my affiliate link? Would anyone take the time and money to sign up for my registration? These will never be answered until someone does notice you and shell out money to buy from you. The significance of that first sale for any business cannot be underestimated. It is considered a turning point of your venture. A sale, no matter how small, is a proof that you can indeed continue traveling the direction you are currently taking.

If you have not made a sale yet, make it your ultimate goal to make one no matter how long it takes. Having to work and wait for it can be demoralizing and disheartening, especially if you think you have done everything that was written on the book. Seeing no immediate results from your efforts can make you lose heart and want to give up. But it is not true that your efforts are going nowhere because you are in fact creating a strong foundation for your business. You are slowly driving people to your site so they will eventually purchase whatever it is you are offering.

The three most important elements of making a sale online are creating content, getting people to read the content and turning those readers into potential customers. Of course, it would take more work and ingenuity when you put these three into action. You need the right strategies and the right people to target. But you don't need sophisticated technology to do this. Keep your focus and make your goal attainable. Aim for what is important first and everything else will follow suit.

First Steps on How to Make Your First Sale Online

Many people are interested in internet marketing these days because of so many advertisements that are telling people how profitable it is. They say that it is easy to start an internet marketing business. People who start the business however say that things are never easy and it's difficult even to make the first sale. People who say it's easy can say so because they have all the knowledge that beginners do not have. They are familiar to the system that those who are just starting out do not have an idea about.

How to make your money online is the first and for some the most difficult part of the internet marketing business. Once you make the first sale the second and the rest are all easy. As a beginners your focus therefore in internet marketing should be on how to make your first sale online. Although this is not easy there are practical tips that experts would tell to those who would like to start it all out.

1. Ask people, especially those who have experienced the first sale. This can be done by going to internet marketing forums where business-minded people, beginners and experts alike gather. You would learn from these people. Those who have just started are excited to tell others about their accomplishments and those who have been there long enough knows how to encourage those who have tried and failed.

2. Don't hesitate to try. Once knowledge is learned, it should be realized by trying it out practically. Hesitation is the biggest hindrance to the first sale. Those who want to have their first sale should be bold enough to start.

Things To Do Before You Make Your First Sales Call

Imagine you are making your first sales call with the intention of selling a financial product or service to a potential client. This can be a truly daunting task! You are likely to have conversations with "Gatekeepers", PA's, EA's, Switchboard operators and other staff who do not have the authority to purchase your product or service in the first place. In addition you may be delaying them from doing their daily work and adding to their stress levels. This may lead to them refusing to take the telephone conversation any further and have the effect of impacting on your self-confidence too.

Now, I don't know about you, but I heard many children's stories when growing up that have a moral or teaching point embedded in them. One that springs to mind is that of Robert the Bruce, who despite losing many battles with the English, finally won freedom for Scotland. The moral being: try, try and try again until you succeed.

This may seem like a good moral story, however, in the field of business or indeed life, this could be disastrous. The word "try" itself implies failure. If you are "trying" to do something you are not actually doing it! If you are trying to win, this implies you are losing. If you think back to how many times you may have heard the phrase "I will really try to make it". Now compare this with the phrase "I will definitely be there". They're worlds apart, aren't they?

In business, yes you can try things but if they do not work you must try something else until you find one that works. Alternatively, you can learn from others mistakes and utilize techni ues that have a higher success rate than others. Simply trying without gauging results is like watching a movie several times and expecting a different result each time.

It is a fact that it is getting harder and harder to talk to the right decision maker/buyer, especially in a larger organization. You have to remember that people are busier than they have ever been at work. The key decision makers are normally the busiest, running from meeting to meeting, so catching them may be extremely difficult.

Below, I have listed some of the main things to do before you even consider making your first sales call to a company:

Research: Before making your first sales call you must research the organization thoroughly. Looking at the company's website is a good start. It can give you a good idea of the organizational structure however you may still not get the names of individuals you re uire to make your sale.

Human Resources Department: Most of the larger organizations have a Human Resources department. This is the key department to contact and simply talking to one of the HR team can give you valuable insight into the buying power of key individuals within the organization.

Offer Value: Every time you contact a member of staff regardless of who they may be you should ensure that you enhance that person's day rather than add to their work pressures. Simply by talking politely to them or using a little humor may be enough. For others a free report that is relevant to the work they do. Become known in the company for being helpful and distinguish yourself from your competitors.

Belief in your products or services: It is important for you to believe in your own product or services. If you can show a client in a totally congruent way that your product or service can solve an actual problem or issue that they have, they are more likely to want to speak to you.

Position yourself in the market place: Be seen as the industry specialist. A potential client is more likely to contact you if you are a perceived expert in solving their problems.

Use different types of communication: There are a number of different mediums you can use: fax, mail, postcards, CD's/DVD's, email, invitation for a free coffee at a local coffee house. The idea is to be creative so that you are not considered to be the same as your competitors.

After you have laid the groundwork by utilizing the above, then it's time to consider making your first sales call. By this time you should have a real feel for the business and the people working for it. At this stage you may have a few contacts in the company who could recommend your services to the key decision maker, or at the very least you will be aware of who the key decision maker is.

Main Things To Consider Before Making Your First Sales Call To A Company:

- ❖ *Research*
- ❖ *Human Resources Department*
- ❖ *Offer Value*
- ❖ *Belief in your products or services*
- ❖ *Position yourself in the market place*
- ❖ *Use different types of communication*

CHAPTER FIVE

ENJOYING YOUR FIRST SALE

So now that you have finally made a sale you have a understanding about how everything works. See it wasn't that hard was it? Well while you were putting things on you were probably wondering how in the heck are people getting that many things online. Well if you were this lesson will definitely help you out.

The first tool that you will need to download is Turbo Lister from eBay

This tool is totally free and will really speed up your listing. It is extremely easy to use and I suggest that you play around with a little bit before you start putting it to work.

So to start, create a account. This account will link to your eBay account.

After you do this you can start listing and start listing fast. You can save all your setting so if you have the same priced items you can save all of that information and only have to type in the description, title, category and picture and you are done. So play around with it and you will start understanding it better. I will give you more tips for the Turbo Lister in later blogs.

So if you have already sold all of your items from around the house then your probably wonder where to find more products to sell. Well I am going to give you some of my simple ideas of finding stuff to put online.

My favorite places to go to find very cheap items is to go to a thrift store. There are many well-known ones like Goodwill,

Salvation Army (the cheapest) and there are also going to be a lot of small privately owned stores as well. I recommend Salvation Army and go on Wednesdays because everything is half off.

So what are you going to be looking for when you go? The easiest and best thing to do is clothes. You spend 100 bucks and get 50-60 items of clothes and make 300-400 bucks off of easy. Now if you don't want to spend that much it is fine. Spend as much as you feel fit.

The brand of clothes are very important. I would go with the American Eagle, Abercrombie and those types of clothes. They are the most sought after clothes on eBay and you can get these at a thrift store for about 2 to 3 bucks a pop. Always check your clothes before you buy them for rips, holes, missing buttons, and stains.

That's the downside of buying thrift, not all the clothes are in perfect condition.

Next after you have looked around for clothes they always just have things sitting around that are brand new. This is where you have to think outside the box. You never know what you can find in these thrift store that will sell for 200% more online. You just have to put in some work. Remember selling on eBay is a job. Think of it like a job and you will make money. If you think of it as a easy money source then you won't make that much.

So your back home now and you're ready to get your treasures on the eBay. Well here is a valuable tip to follow. Because I know the prices of the clothes that you bought at this place I can tell you what you should price them at. I know that these seem low but you will sell them fast and make more money. If you price them too high you will risk not selling them at all. So just follow this guideline or clothes that you buy at Salvation Army. If you bought them at another thrift shop use the same guidelines. My guidelines below go off of t-shirts being $0.50 Button Downs $2.00 and jeans being $4.00. So if you bought them at another place for more then you can just mark them up according. If you have any ⬚uestions you can message me directly for ⬚uestions.

PRICING GUIDE

- T-shirts - $2.99 - $4.99 and $5.99 S&H
- Button Down - $4.99 - 6.99 and $5.99 S&H
- Jeans - 7.99 - 9.99 and 7.99 S&H

Use that to price your clothes and I will explain why. T-shirts you will always send out first class mail. They will cost about 2-3 bucks to send. So now you can calculate your profit. $0.50 for shirt and approx. 2.50 to send. That makes 3 bucks. Well you are making approx 6 bucks IF only ONE person bids on them. So time that by how many t-shirts you have and you have your potential profit. See how that can add up ⬚uickly. You can use that same math to figure out your other categories. You can try other pricing guides but this has worked for me. My biggest tip is to not overprice the items. Of course you have a really nice Abercrombie shirt that cost 30 bucks in their store. But people don't get on eBay to buy at the store price. They're looking for a deal so price it low get rid of it and make your profit.

So you didn't buy just clothes. Let's say you found a brand new coffee maker in the store for 7 bucks. Well this is where some research will have to go into place. You will need to go to eBay and sign in. Type in the exact name of the coffee maker to see if they're selling and what they're selling it. So once you have done all of this scroll down and press completed. You may also want to click the new only tab to and find the new ones selling. So you see that it's selling for about 25 bucks. (this is all made up in my head so don't take it for fact) Well then I would price it for about 14.99 and 19.99 and about 8.99 shipping and handling. Why not price it at 25 bucks? Because if you price it just a little bit lower then the chances of it selling doubles. So you make sure you make money out of it.

There are many tools out there to simplify this process. I would suggest in buying a smartphone. Not just any smartphone but one that will scan bar codes. This will tremendously help you find good products. If you already have one with these capabilities then you need to go to your app store and download 3 or 4 scanners. They all will help in some way. My favorite is the Amazon Scanner.

I like this scanner because Amazon has the biggest inventory of products online. All of these products have description and photos that you can use for your eBay listings. So that coffee maker you could have scanned into your phone. When you got home add that product to your wish list via the scanner and you have all the information you need about that product. This saves time trying to find it on the box or searching for it.

So now that you know all of this, get out there and find your items and get them online. Yeah if your looking at this and saying it seems like work. Well it is. Just because your working from home doesn't mean that you are not working. So get at there and look hard. Put in the time if your doing it full time put in 40 hours a week if it's part-time put in 15 -20. If you do this you will make money.

Sales Training - Remember Your First Sales Success

Imagine the novelty of steam-powered brass machines getting to the first USA automobile show in the snow! Then imagine the newness of making your first sale. Getting that first or first few sales is tough but exhilarating. Think back to that first success and find the basic elements.

Then when you need to gain a boost or reestablish your confidence you take that first ride once again.

Warm up. Just like the old brass cars needed time to warm up, it's likely on your first call you rehearsed out loud, or at least mentally, your opening presentation. You carefully planned what you would take along to the meeting - just in case you needed a brochure or a price estimate.

Open the door. In building rapport, you found it easiest to be observant and to make genuine, caring comments on your observations in your prospect's office or home.

Get in and sit. With the rapport building all warmed up, you began to ask ☐uestions to go deeper in learning about your prospect's needs and wants.

Start the car. As you discover what your client needs and wants you qualify them as the decision maker, when and how they will decide to buy, and how much and how they will purchase. You know that unless you are on a flat surface with the prospect, to begin any presentation may possibly be a waste of theirs and your time.

Get moving and navigating the turns. When you find the prospect is ready, your presentation revolves around their stated interests, not just yours. The benefits are the benefits that they uncovered for you during the start of your conversation, not the ones you want to talk about.

Going faster. Just as there are shift points even in the oldest of cars, there are shift points in a sales conversation. You take your lead from the driver, the prospect. If they want to go slower, you slow down; if they give you an indication they are ready to decide, you gently guide them to that point to buy from you.

Stop and park the car. Stopping is actually the beginning of the sale.

Remember how you felt when the first client shook your hand? Remember how it felt when you made the first delivery or shipment? You wouldn't downshift if you were in high gear in a car, so don't slow the process down by ignoring or overlooking that the prospect is ready to decide.

That first car show may not be something people alive can fully relive. However, a salesperson who relives the thrill of their first sale will find the experience enough to feel a successful move through the process at any time. Just take a mental ride back in your history to remind yourself of what goes into the plan and approach.

Remember Your First Sales Success reestablish your confidence you take that first ride once again.

- ❖ *Warm up.*
- ❖ *Open the door.*
- ❖ *Get in and sit.*
- ❖ *Start the car.*
- ❖ *Get moving and navigating the turns.*
- ❖ *Go faster.*

CHAPTER SIX

4 CRUCIAL THINGS YOU NEED WHEN BUILDING YOUR LIST

Internet website marketing has sustained a sudden rise these past few years. As more internet based companies are established, the desire to cultivate new marketing and advertising expertise and knowledge determined by this new medium have arisen. More and more marketing approaches are being discovered and developed to address the altering face of business in the world.

Opt-in marketing calls for the consent of an enthusiastic consumer to subscribe to your advertising and marketing materials, materials that take appearance in newsletters, catalogs and promotional mailings by means of e-mail. The more opt-in marketing mail is distributed, the more likelihood there exists to bag sales plus much more income. To perform this, you must build a catalog of all people that wish to subscribe to your email marketing list.

Lots of people can think that building their lists would take working hard plus a lot of time to gain and collect names and addresses. And that is just not so, it takes some persistence and some methods but in doing this, you open your site and your business to a complete new world of target market. Make the trouble to take your business to an extra height, if increased traffic and good income are what you want, an opt-in list can perform miracles for your online business enterprise.

Now a few ideas to help you when building your list:

1) Set up an effective web form on your site that instantly follows the end of your content. While some may utter this is

often ahead of time to ask for a website visitors registration, aim to remember that your homepage needs to offer a □uick first-class impact.

2) As pointed out in the first idea, create your homepage to be very, very striking. You will need to boast well-written articles or reviews and descriptions of your web site. Depending on exactly what your web site is all about, you will want to capture your website visitor's fancy. Make your site to be useful and very straightforward to make use of and this will help greatly in building your list.

3) Supply good service and products. A come back purchaser is more liable to bring in additional dealing. A content consumer will recommend a business all the time. Word of mouth and recommendations unaided can rake in more trade than an expensive classified ad. As your customer roster gets bigger so will your list. Along with new members on your list, the more people can get to find out about what you have new to present.

4) Maintain a fresh and personal register when building your list. Never lose the trust your clients have entrusted you. If you ever give e-mail addresses from your list to other marketers and your clients get spammed, many may unsubscribe to you.

Bear in mind, a solid status will guide in additional traffic and subscribers as well as strengthen the devotion of your customers.

Selling For Beginners

Most sales training courses are based on one or two well-practiced theories of selling.

The selling circle, which is a 12 step system that takes you through the whole process, and works on the principle that you never move to the next step until, you have closed the door of the step you are working on. In other words it does not allow the flexibility to backtrack on any part of the sales presentation, this I feel to be a little too complicated for the novice.

The second popular system is known as FAB selling, this stands for Features and Benefits. This technique is probably the most popular and the easiest to teach to a newcomer. It bases its theory on the fact every product has a number of features, which the salesperson will learn by heart. With each feature comes a benefit to the purchaser, this works well in a lot of situations but is lost in others.

The system that I find is the most effective for most apprentice salespeople would be, the 4 'I's and this the one I am going to explain now

1. Ice breaker; this is the most important part of any sales presentation. You need to find a common interest or to get the prospect "on side" relaxed and open-minded. The way you position yourself during the meeting, your body posture and the words you use at this point can make or break the deal. Use the parrot technique - if they are using familiar terminology like buddy or pal, then you use the same. Try to get some humor into the ice breaker, but be careful and only if the "parrot" allows.

2. Identify the problem; it is a common misconception to think we purchase stuff just for the sake of it. We don't, 90% of the time we are looking for a solution to a particular problem. Your job at this stage is to identify that problem and grind it down. Don't take the first response given, you have two ears

and one mouth, use them in that ratio and listen, then listen some more. Find the underlying problem as to why you have been invited there. Let's just look at some examples - you buy a hamburger, why? The problem was you were hungry. You buy an SUV, why? Problem is you've got 3 kids that need to get to school and the disco on Friday night. The issue here is we all buy things every day, but when you look closely at the motive (the buying motive) it will nearly always be some kind of problem that the purchase has fixed. So we spend as much time as it takes to identify the correct problem.

3. Introduce the solution; this is where the fun comes in. You need to show the purchaser how what you are selling will solve the problem they have.   Sometimes it needs a few little statements to make them realize what a pain it would be if they don't purchase what you are offering. For example, if you are selling a dining table and chairs, you may say, "so Mrs. Smith, where do you sit for your family meals right now?" The reply may be something like, we sit on the couch in front of the TV, "how does that make you feel?" You are looking for, emotion - feelings play a huge role in purchasing anything. The two main emotive reasons to buy are, distress and desire, which one is it? You can find out by asking key ⬚uestions and you listen to the reply, listen.

Once you have established the buying motive you can offer the solution to the problem. Again, the example may be "so Mrs. Smith, if I can show you an affordable way, you and your family are able to sit together, around this beautiful table for your meals, then I take it, it would be of interest to you? At this point you are looking for a positive reply, you need a "yes"

If you don't get one you go back and look for the real problem, and then you ask again. If you have found the correct problem and you ask the correct question, you will get a "yes".

OK, you are half way to a sale now. At some time during your presentation you need to do what's called price conditioning, this is where you try to get an idea of what the customer thinks your product is worth to them.

There are several ways this can be done, but the most simple is to just ask what the budget is, they will tell you. If it is in the ballpark of what you are selling that's good news, if what you are offering is more than the budget, then you need to spend a little more time in building the worth of your product. Show them how this purchase will not only solve the problem they have now, but will help prevent a problem that may arise a bit later, most of the time purchasers will find a bit more in their wallet, practically if you have made the distress purchase become a desire one, or the desire one even more desirable.

4. Invite the sale; you need to ask for the business. So Mr. Brown, will you want 3 or 4? OK Mrs. Smith we can have it delivered Wednesday, is AM or PM better for you? Shall we get the paperwork started, we can do a 10% deposit and the rest on delivery is that OK or would you rather pay all now? Or something as simple as, so Mr. Cole, can we do business? However you ask, make sure you do ask.

Always remember, selling doesn't start until the prospective purchaser says no, the more no's you get the closer to a yes you are getting. Don't get downhearted, always stay positive and you must believe in your product with a passion. Don't lie, don't exaggerate and remember to always under promise, and over deliver on what you are offering, good luck.

Now you have a few ideas to help you when building your list:

❖ *Set up an effective web form on your site that instantly follows the end of your content.*

- *As pointed out in the first idea, create your homepage to be very, very striking.*
- *Supply good service and products.*
- *Maintain a fresh and personal register when building your list.*

CONCLUSION

Thank you again for downloading this book!

I hope this book was able to help you to acquire all necessary set of skills so that you can run and make your first sale smoothly.

So there you have it; *"How to Sell For Beginners: The First Guide You Need To Make Your First Sale"*. Always remember that it's best to be prepared before jumping into tasks at hand to make sure that you do your research first before diving into any business decisions. Though it may seem a bit confusing at first, don't get easily intimidated, as there are always experts that you can turn to for advice.

The next step is to target the right people and you need the right strategies. But you don't need sophisticated technology to do this. Keep your focus and make your goal attainable. Aim for what is important first and everything else will follow suit.

Finally, if you enjoyed this book, then I'd like to ask you for a favor, would you be kind enough to leave a review for this book on Amazon? It'd be greatly appreciated!

Thank you and good luck!

www.ingramcontent.com/pod-product-compliance
Lightning Source LLC
Chambersburg PA
CBHW030737180526
45157CB00008BA/3206

* 9 7 8 1 0 9 2 8 1 4 9 0 4 *